P9-EER-618

JERRY YANG

AND

DAVID FILO

THE FOUNDERS OF YAHOO!®

T 31891
L

INTERNET CAREER BIOGRAPHIES™

JERRY YANG

AND

DAVID FILO

THE FOUNDERS OF YAHOO!

MICHAEL R. WESTON

The Rosen Publishing Group, Inc., New York

Published in 2007 by The Rosen Publishing Group, Inc.
29 East 21st Street, New York, NY 10010

Copyright © 2007 by The Rosen Publishing Group, Inc.

First Edition

All rights reserved. No part of this book may be repro-
duced in any form without permission in writing from
the publisher, except by a reviewer.

Library of Congress Cataloging-in-Publication Data

Weston, Michael R.
Jerry Yang and David Filo: the founders of Yahoo!/
Michael R. Weston.—1st ed.
       p. cm.—(Internet career biographies)
Includes bibliographical references and index.
ISBN 1-4042-0718-X (library binding)
1. Yang, Jerry—Juvenile literature. 2. Filo, David—
Juvenile literature. 3. Yahoo! Inc.—History—Juvenile
literature. 4. Internet industry—United States—
Juvenile literature. 5. Businesspeople—United
States—Biography—Juvenile literature.
I. Title. II. Series.
HD9696.8.U62Y364 2007
338.7'6102504092273—dc22

                                        2005030125

Manufactured in the United States of America

On the cover: Jerry Yang *(left)* and David Filo *(right)*.

Contents

If you listen closely, you can hear the sound of progress. It's the sound heard in the hum of a hard drive or the shuffling of a chair, the tapping of a keyboard or the sliding of a mouse. It is the sound of modern, twenty-first-century communication.

This sound—of people using the Internet to conduct business, play games, send e-mail, pay bills, rent DVDs, and surf thousands of Web sites—is a recent one. Through the early 1990s, most people had never used e-mail or logged on to an Internet account. College students did all their research in libraries, where they leafed through books and journals. Phone numbers were found in phone books. Letters were mailed through the post office. News was gathered from newspapers, radio broadcasts, or through television newscasts; it was definitely not found online.

The digital age is marked by speed and efficiency. Today, if you have access to a computer and the means to connect to the Internet, you also have access to a nearly endless supply of information. This information is stored on

David Filo (left) and Jerry Yang (right) are true Internet pioneers. They've led one of the Internet's most successful businesses into the twenty-first century and have no plans to let up. Yang and Filo set the pace for the Internet revolution by blazing a new path in e-commerce and especially in search engine technology. Expect to see Yang and Filo on the cutting edge of Internet commerce for many years to come.

other computers and is sent to you as code over phone lines or cable lines, or through a wireless connection. Your computer deciphers the coded information, translating it into something you can easily recognize.

Some people say that modern history can be divided into two distinct periods: the period before the Internet and the period occurring now. Although everyone may not agree with this, it's impossible to deny one fact: the Internet has been nothing short of revolutionary. It has changed the way the world works, and modern life would not be the same without it.

The Internet has revolutionized the way we communicate, and it has spawned a generation of entrepreneurs. These entrepreneurs have generally been young men and women who grew up in just the right time and place and have taken advantage of every opportunity that has come their way. Through their visionary thinking, these people—inventors, innovators, scientists, engineers, businesspeople, and others—have made the Internet what it is today.

Jerry Yang and David Filo, the creators of the Internet portal and search engine Yahoo!, are two such visionaries. They jumped headfirst into the online fray over a decade ago, risking their

JULY 20, 1998 $2.95

www.time.com

TIME

KISS YOUR MALL GOODBYE

Online shopping is faster, cheaper and better

Plus: Hot stocks and brash billionaires

Jerry Yang
of Yahoo!

In 1998, Jerry Yang surfed the Internet boom all the way to the cover of *Time* magazine. Yang and Filo worked hard to make Yahoo! more than just a search engine. With more and more people going online to do their shopping, Yahoo! was in the right place to take perfect advantage of the trend.

degrees, their careers, and their reputations for a chance at success.

Yang and Filo put everything on the line, but it paid off big in the end. The two young men created an extremely successful business, which made them millionaires virtually overnight. They became celebrities and have been profiled in magazines and interviewed on radio and television. With their innovations, they've influenced the direction the Internet has taken in ways that no one else has. They've changed the way that people view information, and they've changed the way the world does business. They're still going strong after ten years, and they've never looked back.

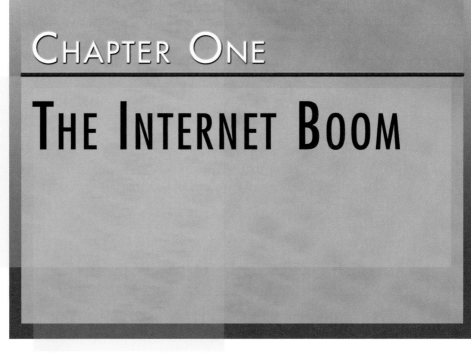

CHAPTER ONE

THE INTERNET BOOM

The story of Yahoo! and its founders, Jerry Yang and David Filo, begins with the creation of the Internet. Like most Internet pioneers, Yang and Filo took advantage of an infrastructure that was already in place. They didn't invent the Internet. They just made it a whole lot easier to navigate.

A GALACTIC NETWORK

By most accounts, the Internet was first conceived in August 1962. It was then that

J. C. R. Licklider, a computer scientist at the Massachusetts Institute of Technology in Boston, came up with an idea for a so-called Galactic Network. Computer scientists before him had worked on finding a way for two computers to communicate, but no one had gone as far as Licklider. The Galactic Network, as Licklider envisioned it, would be a global network of computers. Each computer in the network, no matter where it was located, would have the capacity to communicate with any other computer in the network. A person seated before a computer in Bangkok, Thailand, for example, would be able to contact a computer in San Francisco, California. If it worked, as Licklider expected it would, the Galactic Network would revolutionize communication. There was just one problem: where to begin?

ARPA

As luck would have it, President Dwight D. Eisenhower had recently organized a new agency at the U.S. Department of Defense called the Advanced Research Projects Agency (ARPA). ARPA was created in response to the Soviet Union's October 4, 1957, launch of *Sputnik I*, the world's first artificial satellite. At this time in

The world's first artificial satellite, *Sputnik I*, was launched by the Soviet Union in 1957. *Sputnik I* was no bigger than a basketball, but its impact on the world was tremendous. While the Soviets celebrated their first victory in the space race, leaders in America panicked. It was clear that the United States had a lot of work to do if it hoped to catch up.

history, the United States and the Soviet Union were bitter rivals. Although neither side engaged the other in direct military conflict, the threat of war loomed for decades. This tense period of time was known as the Cold War, and it lasted from 1947 until the breakup of the Soviet Union in 1991. During this time, both sides amassed huge stockpiles of weapons, including nuclear weapons, in an attempt to achieve military supremacy.

Not surprisingly, the launch of *Sputnik* scared Eisenhower. If the Soviets could send a satellite into space, what else were they capable of? Were they really that far ahead of the United States when it came to technology? The so-called space race—a battle between the United States and the Soviet Union for the upper hand in space exploration and technology—was on.

President Eisenhower took *Sputnik* as a warning and decided it was time for the United States to get to work. ARPA's purpose was to focus on technological advancement. The agency hired some of the smartest people in the country and gave them the funds and facilities they needed to conduct their research. One of the technologies they would concentrate on was computer networking and communications—the type of technology that could prove very useful in the event of a military conflict with foreign powers like the Soviet Union. They needed someone to run the show, and they found their man in J. C. R. Licklider.

For Licklider, the position at ARPA was perfect. It would allow him to push for the kinds of technological developments necessary to create his Galactic Network. For ARPA, having Licklider at the helm would also be advantageous. A network of the sort he imagined could prove useful in all kinds of military operations. In the following years—the early 1960s—ARPA invested money and resources to develop just such a network.

THE FIRST CONNECTION

Once the ball started rolling at ARPA, it took several years for the research to produce substantial results. In 1965, all the waiting finally paid off. It was then that two researchers, an MIT scientist named Lawrence Roberts and a man named Thomas Merrill, proved it was possible to connect two computers on opposite sides of the country. Using a low-speed dial-up telephone line, they linked a computer in Massachusetts with another in California.

The connection, while a tremendous achievement, was also flawed. It worked, but just barely. Yes, two computers could make contact with one another, and therefore at least the simplest of networks was feasible. But true communication would have to wait. The problem, it seemed, was the path the connection took. The telephone lines used what is called circuit-switching technology. While circuit-switching technology may have been fine for a telephone conversation, it wouldn't do for a conversation between computers.

PACKETS VERSUS CIRCUITS

Circuit-switching technology works like this: When one person calls another person, a circuit, or connection, is created between the two telephones. The connection occurs along a series of linked wires, the telephone lines, that run between the phones. As long as the connection is sustained, no one else can use those specific wires. The circuit is broken when the callers hang up, at which point the wires become available for other users.

Dr. Leonard Kleinrock, inventor of an information-transfer technology critical to the Internet, was right in the middle of it all when the first Internet connection was established. His host computer at the University of California–Los Angeles (UCLA) was one of the four originals used for the ARPANET.

Circuit switching is great for a typical telephone call, but when computers are on either end of the line, things get bogged down. Too much information is crammed into too small a space when a computer tries to send information over a circuit-switched telephone line. All this data needs extra room to travel.

To solve this problem, scientists began investigating an alternative information-transference technology called packet switching. Packet switching, a technique first conceived by a scientist named Leonard Kleinrock, is a process by which information is broken up into small units, or packets, before it is sent. Containing a small amount of the overall information being transferred, each packet is "addressed" to a specific destination so it can be delivered to the right place. The packets can travel along different lines, so as not to bog down one line with too much data. When the packets arrive at their destinations, they are automatically reassembled into one complete message.

Packet switching was still just a theory in 1965. It had never been put to the test. But once the experimental computer network hit a wall because of the limits of circuit switching, it was clear that packet switching would have to become a reality.

Roberts, the MIT scientist involved in that experiment, moved to ARPA in 1966 to spearhead the effort. His goal was to use packet-switching techniques in the development of the world's first version of the Internet: the ARPANET.

THE **ARPANET**

By late 1969, Roberts and his colleagues had the
ARPANET up and running. The earliest form of
this packet-switching network connected four
host computers. Three of the computers were at
locations in California: the Stanford Research
Institute (SRI); the University of California–Santa
Barbara; and the University of California–Los
Angeles. The fourth was located at the University
of Utah.

In the years that followed, the ARPANET
expanded as more and more computers were
added to the network. By the summer of 1970,
the network had grown to include not only the
four original hosts in California and Utah but
also computers at places like MIT, Harvard, and
a private Massachusetts-based company called
BBN. Before long, numerous colleges, government agencies, and private companies from
across the country had joined the group and
become part of the network.

Still, the ARPANET remained relatively
unknown. Personal computers were not available
in the early 1970s. Computers were typically
found only at universities, libraries, high-tech

The Cray supercomputer, built in the late 1970s by Seymour Cray, was one of the world's first truly powerful computers and was among the fastest computers on earth at that time. Today, modern Cray supercomputers are used to solve the most difficult scientific and mathematical problems, such as weather forecasting and climate prediction, quickly and efficiently.

companies, and research facilities. Those who had access to computers linked to the network first had to learn how to use it, and using the network was a complicated ordeal. Nevertheless, the ARPANET was finally put on display for the public to see at the International Computer Communications Conference in 1972. The technology for what would become the Internet had arrived.

E-MAIL

Something else happened in 1972 that would forever change the way the world communicates: electronic mail—better known as e-mail—was invented.

E-mail was created out of necessity. The people behind the ARPANET wanted a way to "talk" with one another through the network, so they developed special software to make it possible. The software allowed them to electronically send and receive written messages, forward messages to other readers, file them away for future reference, and even send one message to many different people at the same time. The system was simple: The writer would compose his message and then send it to a central computer, called a mail server, that was part of the network. The message would then be stored at the

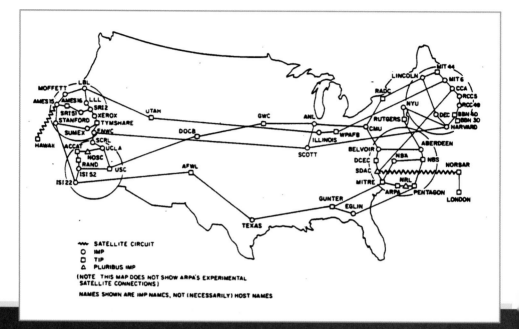

🎧 By 1977, the ARPANET's web of connections linked dozens of major universities, technology companies, and military facilities in the United States. With the ARPANET, a student at Rutgers University in New Jersey could fire off an e-mail to a friend at the University of Southern California and expect it to get there in the blink of an eye.

mail server until the intended recipient logged on to retrieve it. In essence, the mail server acted like a post office, holding the mail until somebody picked it up.

GROWING

From its humble beginnings as a small network consisting of just a few university-operated computers, the ARPANET took off. More and more people logged on to the network to share information and send e-mail. A new computer language called FTP was developed to handle ARPANET's increased traffic. FTP, which stands for file transfer protocol, made it possible to transfer files from one computer to another. A similar language called TCP/IP (transmission control protocol/Internet protocol) was also developed. With FTP and TCP/IP, information could be shared like never before. In fact, both programs are still in use today.

As the years went by, however, it became clear that one issue had yet to be resolved. With so many new network sites appearing all the time, it was becoming harder and harder to keep track of them. People could log on to the network and go to sites they knew of, but they had no idea how to find sites that they weren't familiar with. The network needed to be organized.

THE FIRST ORGANIZING ATTEMPTS

Computer scientists at McGill University in Montreal, Canada, made the first substantial attempt at organizing Internet sites in 1989. The software they developed, nicknamed "Archie," automatically archived (that is, collected and filed) new Internet sites as they appeared. Once a site was archived, it could then be searched for specific files. Archie was useful, but it wasn't for everybody. To use the software, you had to know how to use a computer operating system called UNIX. UNIX was made for computer programmers and was not easy to learn.

Around the same time Archie came into use, researchers developed a software application called the Wide Area Information Server, or WAIS. WAIS allowed Internet users to search more than 600 databases of full-text files from around the world. Like Archie, WAIS was difficult for the average person to use.

INTO THE '90s

In 1991, computer scientists at the University of Minnesota created a system called Gopher (named for the school mascot, the Golden Gopher). Gopher, unlike its predecessors, was very easy to use. You didn't need special computer skills to make it work. Unfortunately, Gopher had one major limitation: it could only be used to find files on the University of Minnesota campus. Still, Gopher was a great search engine, and it was quickly replicated by other software engineers around the world.

Before long, there were thousands of "gophers" in use worldwide, all designed for searching local networks. The next innovation, then, was only logical: a program that could collect all the various gophers from around the world, organize them into a list, and then allow Internet users to search them all at once.

The software that made this possible came from the University of Nevada in Reno. The program was called VERONICA, which stood for "Very Easy Rodent-Oriented Netwide Index to Computerized Archives." VERONICA used what its creators called a spider. The spider, a software robot of sorts, acted like a search engine. By following every link it found, it roamed the Internet in search of gopher menus. When the spider found a menu, it entered the menu into a central index. That index, in turn, could be searched by anyone using VERONICA to navigate the Internet.

Meanwhile, even as other search engines appeared and existing search engines were refined to make them more efficient, a small team of scientists focused on another challenge. In Geneva, Switzerland, scientists at the European Laboratory for Particle Physics were hard at work developing what would eventually become known as the

In the late 1980s and early 1990s, Tim Berners-Lee worked at CERN (Conseil Européen pour la Recherche Nucléaire), the world's largest particle physics laboratory. He realized that CERN's many employees were often unaware of what others at the facility were doing and were therefore unable to share information with each other. Berners-Lee's innovative work with hypertext, the language of the Web, helped solve this problem.

World Wide Web. They were led by a man named Tim Berners-Lee.

Berners-Lee wanted to figure out a way to access information on another computer without having to log on to it. The World Wide Web was developed to make this possible. Created in 1991, the Web used a special language called hypertext. Hypertext allowed Web designers to imbed links directly into the text of a file. Anyone who read that file would see the imbedded link as an under-lined word or series of words. If they clicked on the underlined text, they would be automatically sent to a related Web page.

In 1992, researchers led by Marc Andreessen at the National Center for Supercomputing Applications (NCSA) at the University of Illinois created a software application called Mosaic. Mosaic was a graphical browser, or a program that allowed users to search the Internet by using graphics, or pictures, in addition to text. Mosaic was a major step forward from programs like WAIS, making it a whole lot easier for the average person to navigate the Internet.

MODERN MOVES AND THE NEW "E-CONOMY"

Since the early 1990s, the Internet has evolved from its original design at ARPA to the sleeker,

CHANGING THE LANDSCAPE WITH NETSCAPE

Marc Andreessen may have been the brains behind Mosaic, but he's most famous for what he did after he left the National Center for Supercomputing Applications. In April 1994, Andreessen founded Netscape Communications Corporation with his partner James Clark. Netscape's major product was Netscape Navigator, a World Wide Web browser. The new business made Andreessen extremely wealthy. It also established him as an Internet pioneer and one of the true innovators of the information age. Andreessen's first true competition in the Web browser business came when Bill Gates's company, Microsoft, developed Internet Explorer in 1995.

Microsoft was the largest software company in the world, and it began taking measures to eclipse Netscape. The company used its considerable resources to make Internet Explorer the default browser for people subscribing to Internet service providers (ISPs) such as CompuServe and America Online (AOL). Microsoft also packaged the software free with its Windows operating system and made a deal to include Internet Explorer with Macintosh computers. Microsoft even pressured certain companies who manufactured PCs to include Internet Explorer on their computers. Netscape Navigator may have been the superior browser, but Netscape could not effectively compete against a monolithic company like Microsoft. Although Microsoft eventually came under fire from the U.S. government for its business practices, it was too late for Netscape. The company never quite recovered.

faster, commerce-focused system it is today.
Whereas once it was strictly a means for government agencies, scientific groups, and universities
to communicate, now it's accessible to much of
the world. The Internet has come to serve as a
symbol of democracy—a place where almost
anything goes. Today, information on almost any
subject is available on the Internet. It is a place

Today, doing e-commerce is second nature for many people.
Online businesses such as eBay make buying and selling easy.
Almost anything anyone could ever want or need can be found
on the Internet.

where everyone can speak their mind or listen to other people speak theirs.

Online business, or e-commerce, is now a fact of twenty-first-century life. A large percentage of people now shop, invest, or bank online. Every day, more and more people accept the Internet as a safe and cost-effective place to conduct routine business. The most obvious advantage of doing business online is convenience. By shopping online, you avoid driving, having to find a place to park, and the frustration that comes with long lines. If you know what you're looking for and you have a fast connection and a credit card, you can purchase everything you need in a matter of minutes.

E-commerce would not be possible without e-businesses. Businesses like Amazon.com and eBay have proven that online retailers can make a substantial profit. Internet service providers have also had great success, beginning with a company called Delphi in 1992. Delphi provided its subscribers with e-mail and Internet access. After Delphi, other ISPs followed suit. Companies like AOL, Prodigy, and CompuServe all offered the same services, adding specific features to help make them more appealing to would-be Web surfers.

Today, anyone can get online through these or any of the other countless ISPs in business. With high-speed access available through cable modems, digital subscriber lines (DSL), and satellite connections, hooking up to the Internet is getting faster and easier.

A NEW SPIRIT

The early days of the Internet would not have been possible without the many bold new innovations of the world's top scientists and most ambitious entrepreneurs. Big advances occur only when people take big chances—and that's exactly what many of those at the start did. Their innovative ideas came at a time when computers finally went mainstream. At one time, computers were immovable beasts that took up entire floors and required many people to operate them. With the innovations of the '70s, '80s, and '90s, they became much more compact. As computers shrunk in size, they also became more powerful and less expensive. The price for a desktop computer dropped to the point where many people could afford one. Laptops, too, became a common accessory. Almost everyone had a computer, had plans to get one, or wanted one.

Meanwhile, as mainstream consumers bought the latest computer gadgetry, the Internet continued to develop behind the scenes. An incredible network was forming, holding all kinds of data—some useful, some not—but a simple, practical way of accessing it had yet to be invented. To change this, it would take someone with ambition, someone with a vision. It would require someone with a new take on how the Internet should be used. In fact, it would require two people—specifically, Jerry Yang and David Filo.

Chapter Two

Early Lives of Yang and Filo

I f you're like most people, you probably had never heard the names Jerry Yang and David Filo before you began reading this book. Yang and Filo are the creators of Yahoo!, one of the most successful companies ever to do business on the Internet. They're not well known outside of the world of computer technology, and that's exactly the way they like it.

Yang and Filo were in the right place at the right time. Any earlier, and they could have gone into a number of alternate careers. Any later, and they would have missed the Internet revolution altogether. As it was, in the early 1990s, Yang and Filo were both in the perfect position to take a chance. They devoted themselves to an Internet start-up company.

So how did they get to that place? How did they find themselves at the helm of one of the world's fastest-growing companies? To learn the answers to these questions, you have to go back to the late 1960s and early 1970s, a time when the Internet was just an experiment. Back to the days when Jerry and David were just kids.

THE EARLY YEARS

Jerry Yang was born in Taiwan. He stayed there until the age of ten, when his family moved to San Jose, California. The third-largest city in California, San Jose is located in what is called Silicon Valley, the center of the computer industry in the United States. Silicon Valley is home to many notable entrepreneurs in the computer industry.

David Filo is from Moss Bluff, Louisiana, a town just east of the Texas border and slightly north of the Gulf of Mexico. It is separated from the gulf by vast marshlands and waterways.

Silicon Valley is the center of the high-tech computer industry. Silicon Valley is bordered by San Francisco Bay to the east, the Santa Cruz Mountains to the west, and the Coast Range to the southeast. Today, many entrepreneurs continue to flock to Silicon Valley to take part in the Internet revolution.

After graduating high school, both Yang and Filo went to college. Filo went to Tulane University in New Orleans, Louisiana, a short drive from his hometown. Yang went to Stanford University in California, where he earned his bachelor of science (BS) degree and master's degree (MS) in electrical engineering in 1990.

SILICON VALLEY

Silicon Valley is a nickname for an area south of San Francisco Bay, encompassing the cities of San Jose and Sunnyvale, where Yahoo! headquarters is located. The name comes from the chemical element silicon, which is used to manufacture computer circuits.

Silicon Valley was born when a man named Frederick Terman, who taught at Stanford University, decided to create a technical community in the area. Many Stanford students moved to urban centers such as Los Angeles after leaving school. Terman didn't want so many graduates to leave the area.

Stanford owned a lot of unused land, and Terman came up with a plan to develop the property. In 1951, Stanford Research Park was created. The park's buildings were rented at low-cost to technical companies. As an added incentive for businesses, Terman attracted investors looking to put their money into new technical companies. Terman's plan worked. Technical companies began springing up right and left.

Silicon Valley would eventually become the center of the electronics and computer industry. Entrepreneurs, including tech-savvy college students like Jerry Yang and David Filo, flocked to the valley, where businesses were experiencing a period of extremely rapid growth. Today, Silicon Valley is home to more millionaires than anywhere else in the United States. Many of those millionaires are retired. Many more continue to work for the businesses that made them rich. Others, looking for more excitement, have started new companies and begun all over again.

Filo, who is two years younger than Yang, earned a BS in computer engineering in 1988. In 1994, he earned a master of science (MS) degree in the same subject.

After getting his degree at Tulane, Filo left New Orleans for California, where he enrolled in Stanford's electrical engineering program. There he continued with his education, eventually earning a master's degree in electrical engineering. After Yang graduated with his master's degree, he, too, decided to stay in school—at Stanford, in fact. As luck would have it, Filo and Yang found themselves at Stanford at the same time, in the same academic department.

Yang and Filo soon became close friends, getting to know each other well at their school's Stanford-in-Kyoto exchange program. The program allowed Stanford graduate students to go to Japan to study at the Stanford Center for Technology and Innovation, or SCTI. It was a cultural exchange program as much as it was an academic program—Yang and Filo not only learned about the latest in technology and engineering but also had the chance to meet other students from different parts of the world. It was a formative experience for the two young men.

Back in California after the exchange, Yang and Filo began slugging away at their doctoral degrees together. They each hoped to earn a Ph.D. in electrical engineering. They were studying electronic computer-aided design and developing ideas on how to improve and automate the production of computer chips.

THE PROBLEM

Filo and Yang worked hard at their studies. They spent long hours at their desks, working with their teachers, and trying to create their dissertations. They both eventually grew tired of the work. They were no longer interested in their classes and were disillusioned with their research. School was becoming a chore, and neither of them really enjoyed it. The thought of writing a thesis—a paper that presents a student's research—was very unappealing.

"I was terribly bored," Filo recalled in an interview with *Metroactive* magazine some years later. In the same article, Yang agreed. "Really," said Yang, "we'd do anything to keep from working on our theses."[1]

In another interview, this time in a 1999 airing of the *Motley Fool Radio Show*, Yang elaborated. "We found every single possible way of distracting ourselves from writing the thesis," he said. "We played golf and played rotisserie fantasy basketball leagues, and through all that experience we were using the Internet to do a lot of our research, and not only for real research, but also for our fantasy basketball and things like that."[2] Yang and Filo did not enjoy graduate school, but they enjoyed their time on the Net.

Finally, the decisive moment came. Yang and Filo's adviser—the faculty professor who acted as a mentor, guiding them through their research—left school to take a sabbatical in Italy. The two men were on their own, and they suddenly had a choice to make. They could continue with what they were doing, or they could do something else.

Gradually drifting away from their academic duties, the two young men devoted more and more time to what was rapidly becoming their shared passion: surfing the Internet. They found the Net, a virtual world with essentially unlimited potential, fascinating.

MOSAIC

Both Yang and Filo had used the Internet in the past—since 1993, in fact. When Mosaic, the program Marc Andreessen of Netscape had invented to help people surf the Net, came out, Yang and Filo were amazed and inspired. Yang recalled the time in that same interview with the *Motley Fool Radio Show*: "Mosaic . . . revolutionized the way people thought about multimedia and

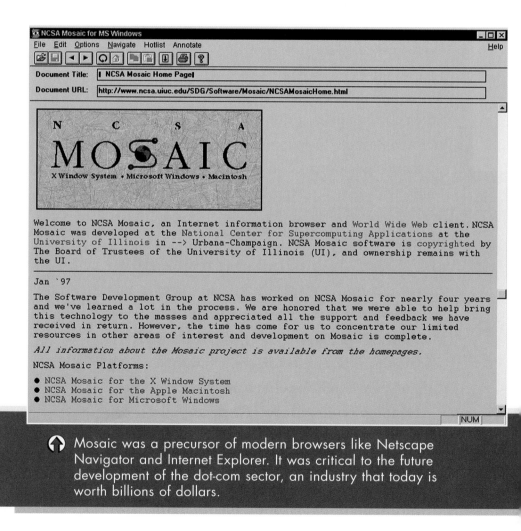

Mosaic was a precursor of modern browsers like Netscape Navigator and Internet Explorer. It was critical to the future development of the dot-com sector, an industry that today is worth billions of dollars.

the Internet," he said. "And we were just like everybody else, totally blown away with the fact that you could now be multimedia-enabled through the Internet."[3]

Filo and Yang, the Stanford boys who were supposed to be studying, rapidly evolved into full-fledge Internet pros. The more they surfed the Internet, the more they realized that it was extremely disorganized. There was no way for them to easily find the sites they wanted to find. And when they did find a site, then leave it, they'd often forget where it was and never find it again. There were lots of great Web sites out there, but there was no way to keep track of them all.

THE SOLUTION

Yang and Filo were engineers by trade, and engineers can be sticklers for perfection. When something is wrong, an engineer will rarely just sit back and ignore the problem. That would solve nothing, and engineers like to solve things.

In January 1994, Yang and Filo decided to do something about the Internet. As engineering students, they wanted something to make it organized and easier to navigate. Rather than wait for someone else to invent the software that would do this, they put their heads together and came up with an idea themselves.

By February, Yang and Filo were off and running. They took the personal computers they used for school, hooked them up in the old Stanford University campus trailer they used as an office, and started surfing the Web. This time, they surfed with a distinct purpose: to find, list, and categorize cool sites. As they surfed, they kept a running tally of every site they visited and where it was located.

"It was the real early days of the Net," Filo told a reporter at *Metroactive* magazine a few years later. "We'd wander around the Net and find something interesting, and then I'd ask Jerry, 'Hey, where was that cool page we saw the other day,' and we could never remember where it was. I mean, it could take us hours to just get back there, to find it. So we made ourselves a hot list, mostly to keep track of little databases and categories."[4]

They categorized each site according to content, then organized them into subcategories to make them even easier to find. Every time a category became too big, they developed new subcategories. Once Yang and Filo had developed a good list, they built a search engine that used key words to find the sites. Everything was listed in http format, which uses hypertext, or point-and-click technology. That made it very easy to navigate to different links.

Yang and Filo made sure to keep things fun as they worked. They even named their workstation computers after famous sumo wrestlers they admired. Yang called his computer, which acted as the Web server, "Akebono." Filo called his, which held the software that made everything run, "Konishiki." The two young men eventually grew so busy cataloging the Internet that school became an afterthought.

So Good, They Had to Share

In April 1994, Yang and Filo posted their list online. At first they called it Jerry's Guide to the World Wide Web, but Yang didn't like the name. It seemed unfair to name it for himself when Filo was doing just as much work on it, so they renamed it. Calling it Jerry and David's Guide to the World Wide Web, their original intention was to put the list up for their friends to use. They hoped it would help them find good sites.

Their friends appreciated the list and used it a lot. Yang and Filo kept working. The number of sites on the list grew all spring, and by the summer they had created a hierarchy of categories to help organize everything and make searching easy. At this point, the guide included nearly 32,000 individual Web pages.

At first, the Yahoo! home page and database contained just a fraction of the listings they do today. Yahoo! also contained no advertisements, as they were not yet accepted as a fair way to make money online. Its streamlined style, with simple, easily searchable topics listed in alphabetical order, was revolutionary for the time.

Still, not many people had heard of the list. Outside of Yang and Filo's close-knit circle of friends, most people were still searching the Net the old-fashioned way. According to an article in the *San Francisco Chronicle*, around this time Yang made an attempt to spread the word by posting a brief message on a Usenet group intended for computer specialists: "We have a pretty comprehensive listing at the Yahoo Database," he wrote, alluding for the first time to what would eventually become the name of their business. "It's an attempt to be organized by subject (although not very well)—but we are working on it."[5]

That message may have helped get the ball rolling. Before long, without any formal advertising on Yang or Filo's part, hundreds of people were using the search engine. As the news got out, mainly by word of mouth, their list became more and more popular.

Earlier that same summer, Yang and Filo had decided to officially rename their search system. Jerry and David's Guide to the World Wide Web just didn't have the flair they were looking for. It was too long and too hard to remember. And Filo, who liked to keep a low profile, didn't like having his name on it.

After a bit of brainstorming, they decided to call it Yahoo!. Recalling his thoughts to the *Metroactive* reporter, Filo was candid. "I was not crazy about the name at first," he said. "But it grew on me."[6]

People have various theories as to what the name symbolizes, but according to Yang and Filo, they pulled it out of a dictionary. So what does it mean? "Rude, unsophisticated, uncouth," say the founders. "'Yahoo' means people who are very uncivilized and rude, and if you get to know us you certainly know that's true," said Yang.[7] The two men also developed a creative description from the letters: "Yet Another Hierarchical Officious Oracle."

GAINING POPULARITY

All through the summer of 1994, the Yahoo! list grew like mad. Yang and Filo put in long hours on the project. They devoted almost all of their time to adding new pages, putting them into appropriate categories, making new categories, and tweaking the search engine to ensure everything worked. Meanwhile, word continued to spread about this new and unique search engine and how much easier it made navigating the Internet. That fall, in fact, Yahoo! saw its first

million-hit day. Nearly 100,000 unique visitors—
each behind his or her own computer screen, each
from his or her own personal little corner of the
world—clicked on the Yahoo! site over 1 million
times that day. Most of them had no idea that
the brains behind Yahoo! were just two graduate
students ignoring their studies.

THE SUITORS ARRIVE

When you develop something as useful as Yahoo!
and you put it online for the world to see, you're
bound to draw some attention. And that's
exactly what happened with Filo and Yang's
business—if it could be called that. They weren't
making any money, nor did they have any intention to. They were just having fun and doing the
world a favor in the process.

Some companies saw Yahoo! in a slightly
different light. Among them were America
Online, Microsoft, and Prodigy. These much
bigger enterprises, with all their money, power,
and influence, repeatedly offered to buy out
Yang and Filo's pet project. They wanted a
piece of the action, and they proposed everything from ownership to partnerships to simple
collaborations. They saw something good, and
they wanted in.

As generous as some of the offers were, Yang and Filo had no interest in being bought out, or at least not yet. They were just doing what they liked to do. They didn't want to sell. They realized the value of what they had developed, but it was too early for them to give Yahoo! away. Besides, they were having too much fun to stop.

Microsoft CEO Bill Gates, speaking via satellite from Washington, addresses television executives and journalists at a 1996 news conference in New York City to announce the launch of the twenty-four-hour NBC-Microsoft news channel. Gates is perhaps the best-known technology pioneer in the world and is by far the richest.

THE PRESSURE'S ON

Meanwhile, Yang and Filo didn't have their own office building at Stanford. They didn't even have jobs. They weren't businessmen, they were electrical engineering students.

So inevitably, as Yahoo!'s traffic increased, their little hobby—the one they started in a campus trailer—outgrew itself and Stanford. Yahoo! was attracting so many Internet users that all the traffic was causing the school's computer system to crash. The school administrators, not surprisingly, didn't like that. Yahoo! was suddenly too big. It needed a new home.

Filo and Yang moved their operation to a nearby company called Netscape Corporation—the same company run by Marc Andreessen. Netscape was designed for sites like Yahoo! It had all the computer capabilities to handle whatever Filo and Yang threw at it. The two grad students said good-bye to Stanford. Netscape would be their new home.

The move to Netscape made Yang and Filo take their site more seriously. Now that they'd left Stanford, they began to think that maybe they should turn Yahoo! into a real business. They knew they had tons of traffic, and people obviously loved their site. Perhaps they could make some money with it.

A First Step

It was probably inevitable that Yahoo! would one day become a real business. And truth be told, Yang and Filo explored the possibilities relatively early on. Their first step was to contact an old college friend of Yang's named Tim Brady.

Filo recalled that move and the others that were soon to follow in an interview for a Stanford University School of Engineering alumni publication. "Thousands of people were producing new Web sites every day," said Filo. "We were just trying to take all that stuff and organize it to make it useful. As it became more popular, it became pretty clear we would have to get more people involved."[8]

Brady was attending Harvard Business School at the time. Yang and Filo thought it might be helpful to have someone like Brady look over their product and help them shape it into a real company. Brady gladly obliged, and before long it was official: Yahoo! was a business. The three men registered the name and incorporated the business on March 2, 1995.

"YAHOO" DEFINED

Gulliver's Travels, written by Jonathan Swift in 1726, is one of the world's great novels and is required reading for many high school students in the United States and around the world. The book, narrated by a fictional doctor and adventurer named Lemuel Gulliver, recounts Gulliver's voyages and mishaps. While considered by many to be a great children's story, *Gulliver's Travels* is a commentary on the follies of human nature. In Swift's book, Yahoos are repulsive creatures with disgusting habits. Since the publication of Swift's novel, "yahoo" has also come to mean a crass or stupid person.

One of Brady's assignments at school was to write up a business plan. Conveniently, Yahoo! needed a business plan of its own, so Brady focused on the new company. He put together an official plan to use as an outline to keep everything moving in the right direction and present to potential investors. The plan was ultimately never used, but it helped the three-man team get organized. They now knew their goals and knew where they wanted to go.

Business in hand, Yang and Filo soon made their first staffing decision. They hired Brady as director of marketing. His job would be to present

Yahoo! to investors in the best light possible. He had to convince them that Yahoo! could make money and was therefore a good company to support.

Brady put together a company prospectus. The prospectus described Yahoo! and the company's plans for the future. Yang and Filo then used the prospectus to shop around for venture capitalists who might be willing to give them money to help the business get started.

IN THE MONEY

Dozens of Silicon Valley venture capitalists showed keen interest in Filo and Yang's proposal. But just one, Mike Moritz of Sequoia Capital, jumped on board. Sequoia Capital was well known in Silicon Valley. Sequoia, and Moritz in particular, had a reputation for funding companies that ultimately became very successful. Apple, Cisco Systems, Atari, and Oracle were among the other businesses Moritz had given money to in their early stages.

At first, though, Moritz was hesitant. He wasn't sure about the name Yahoo!. It sounded a bit childish to him. He was also concerned about the experience—or lack thereof—of the two founders. He wondered if Yang and Filo had what it took to run a business. He wondered if they could actually pull it off.

Still, Moritz knew a winner when he saw one, and he had a hunch about Yahoo!. In April 1995, he put his cards on the table and decided to invest nearly $2 million in the company. It was more than enough to set Yahoo! into motion.

CHAPTER THREE

A BUSINESS IS BORN

With the $2 million in hand, Yang and Filo had everything they needed to get started. Everything, that is, except a workforce.

HIRING TIME

Running a business, especially one with as much potential as Yahoo!, is not an easy job. That job is made even more difficult if you try to do it alone. Yang and Filo realized this, and they knew that they had very little business experience

Noelia Fernandez-Arroyo, senior producer for Yahoo! Spain, sits in her office in Madrid. Today, Yahoo! has offices located worldwide.

between the two of them. They had brought their good friend Tim Brady aboard to put a business plan together, but now they needed more help. They needed hard workers, people they could depend on to get the job done. Most of all, they needed people who understood where the Internet was headed.

Yang and Filo hired old friends they'd known from their school days. They brought on interns—people looking for not just a job but good work experience that would help them land better positions in the future. They also hired experienced businesspeople, such as Jeffrey Mallet, who would be the company's chief operating officer, or COO; and Tim Koogle, a former executive at Motorola and a fellow alumnus of the Stanford Engineering Department. Koogle took over as Yahoo! president and chief executive officer (CEO). As quoted in a Stanford alumni publication, Koogle recalls meeting the two entrepreneurs for the first time and making it clear why he was interested in the job: "What struck me immediately was that they had filled a fundamental need and they had done it intuitively," he said. "That's what you look for in starting a business."[1]

So as not to take themselves too seriously, Yang and Filo took the roles of "Chief Yahoos," and even made business cards with the silly job titles printed on them. It was obvious right from the start that, while this would be a great business, it would also be fun. New titles in hand,

Yahoo! employees, while expected to work hard, are also expected to play. This worker takes a short break to try his hand at an onsite video game while a colleague makes copies. Yang and Filo believe that a happy worker is more productive than one who is not. Yahoo! would not have been as successful as it is today if its employees didn't love their jobs.

the two young men finally cut their ties with Stanford—at least temporarily. They took leaves of absence, put their quests for doctorate degrees on hold, and moved the company headquarters to Mountain View, California, just outside of San Francisco.

Home Sweet Home

The mid-90s were a time of incredible techno-logical innovation and experimentation. Just about everyone who was involved in business had their foot in the door of an Internet start-up, and those who didn't found ways to invest in them through the stock market. It was a wild roller-coaster ride, and people were making lots of money.

For the entrepreneurs, who were risking their money, futures, and reputations, it required mountains of work. Behind the office doors, employees put in ridiculously long hours. They rarely stopped to eat or sleep. When they did manage to get a couple hours of sleep, it was usually behind or underneath a desk. People saw these enterprises as once-in-a-lifetime opportuni-ties. There was a chance to get rich, but it required sacrifice. Many people were more than willing to do whatever it took to succeed.

This Yahoo! employee catches a nap in his Silicon Valley office in March 1997. Long hours broken up by occasional naps were the name of the game in the early years of Yahoo!. Although their work schedule is still demanding, today, employees generally have enough time to go home to sleep.

Those at Yahoo!, for the most part, were no different. Employees put in long, hard hours, eating their meals on the fly and sleeping, if they could, on the office carpet. Twenty-hour workdays were common. Of the two Chief Yahoos, Filo was known to be particularly devoted to his work. Many nights he caught only short spells of sleep on the floor by his desk. Even though he lived just two blocks away, he didn't have the time to go home. He was just too busy.

Despite the early success of the business and the rapidly growing feeling that they were sitting on a gold mine, Filo continued to drive the same beat-up car he had driven in graduate school. In an interview at the time with *Metroactive*, Filo responded to a reporter's question about his car with typical bluntness: "I do

Foosball is a favorite game of Chief Yahoos Yang and Filo. Although Yahoo! was their creation, Yang and Filo didn't let success go to their heads. They were not afraid to have fun at the office and remained normal, everyday guys even after becoming millionaires.

need to get the thing fixed," he said. "But there is just no time."[2]

Much like Filo's car, Yahoo!'s first headquarters were less than perfect. There were three staff members crammed into every office, and each room came with just one phone. There were holes in the roof, and water dripped into the workspace when it rained. Employees were even known to use their trash cans to catch the water and keep it from soaking their desks. Meanwhile, there was the office decor to consider. The Chief Yahoos bought the cheapest purple and yellow paint they could find and splashed the walls with color. In the early days, the people at Yahoo! had little time or money to spare, but they had a whole lot of ambition. And ambition, combined with a great idea, was all they needed.

FIRST THINGS FIRST

Office paint jobs were not the highest priority for the Yahoo! team. It was of utmost importance to get Yahoo! started by sinking money into the things that would guarantee success. The goal was to make the company extremely profitable. Surprisingly, this philosophy was not a given during the start-up craze that was the Internet revolution. Many companies saw profits as merely an added bonus. They were more concerned with appearing to be the next big thing than delivering results. It was not uncommon for the owners of Internet start-up companies to do everything they could to lure a bigger competitor into buying them out. They were less interested in creating a company that would last forever than one that attracted people who would pay them a lot of money. Many companies were founded on great ideas but couldn't make those ideas reality. They were built to make a quick buck; they weren't built to last.

At Yahoo!, though, things were different. Yang and Filo spent money on things that would make the business run. Expensive paint could wait. New and powerful computers could not. This philosophy would ultimately prove critical to Yahoo!'s success. When many dot-coms began to crumble, Yahoo! stood firm. Yahoo! was a business built from the ground up, with an eye toward providing people with what they needed and doing so in a way that made money. Ten years down the road, when many of their competitors were distant memories, Yahoo! would still be standing.

BIGGER AND BETTER

From their somewhat humble beginnings, Yang, Filo, and their new team of workers brought Yahoo! into the big-time world of Internet business. By the summer of 1995, bolstered by a second round of funding that infused the company with more cash, Yahoo! had become a very popular site. Every day, more and more people were turning to the Yahoo! search engine when they needed to find something on the Internet.

People also came to Yahoo! for other things. Thanks to a deal the Yahoo! founders made with Reuters news service, the site now included links to top national and local news stories. Later, the site began offering useful information like stock quotes, weather forecasts, and phone listings. It also posted things like sports scores and links to map-finding services and airline ticketing companies.

Yahoo! quickly evolved into something much more than a search engine. The site became a destination in itself. People made Yahoo! their Internet home page and went to it because it held everything they needed in one place. They could customize the page to fit their interests and needs. Yahoo! was convenient, easy to use, and, most important, free.

It was free thanks to another one of Yang and Filo's savvy business moves. They wanted to bring the company money, but they didn't want

Filo and Yang goof off for the camera in 1997. The fish they are holding was used as a prop in a 1997 television advertisement for Yahoo!. The two are well known in Silicon Valley for not just their success as businessmen but also their commitment to the community. They've put millions of dollars back into their local economy and have made many generous donations, including financial gifts to their old school, Stanford University.

to charge users for basic services. So they decided to sell advertising, and before long they had multiple major companies posting ads on their site. Some of Yahoo!'s earliest sponsors included American Express, British Airways, and Lexus. When they saw the advertising, some people accused Yang and Filo of selling out, but the two founders knew better than that. They weren't selling out. They were giving consumers what they wanted while ensuring that the company made money in the process. They knew that if they were to succeed, they had to have a source of revenue. Advertising was just one way to bring in revenue.

Not surprisingly, it wasn't long before other Internet companies followed Yahoo!'s lead and began offering advertising space of their own. Yahoo! had taken a big chance and pulled it off. Now others followed suit.

GOING PUBLIC

In the mid- to late '90s, "going public" was often a smart business move for Internet entrepreneurs. When a business goes public, it offers members of the public the opportunity to become part owners of the business by purchasing stock in the company. Initial public offerings, or IPOs, put

IPOs

Companies go public with an initial public offering, or IPO. An IPO puts a portion of a company up for sale to the public, or to anyone who can afford to buy it. Typically, the sale is in the form of shares. Shares are sold at a specific price at the IPO. Once they are dispersed, the shares can be freely traded on the stock market.

Stock prices go up and down for a variety of reasons. If a company is doing well, it's likely that more people will want to buy its shares. With that higher demand for shares, the price of a share will tend to increase. On the other hand, as demand for shares decreases, which tends to happen when a company is doing poorly, the price per share may also go down.

Other factors also contribute to a stock's price. The general state of the economy, political events, rumors of company leaders resigning, or even the weather can influence what a stock will fetch on the open market.

shares of a company for sale on the stock market so that anyone can buy them. If the stock value goes up, investors can make a hefty profit by selling their shares at a later date. Buying stock is also risky; if the share prices go down, the value of an investor's holdings go down with them. For businesses, going public means an instant infusion of much-needed cash. And to build a good company into a great one, you need cash.

When people buy shares, the money they spend on those shares goes to the company they are buying the shares from. They essentially give their money to the company in exchange for a slip of paper that gives them part ownership of that company. The company can then take that money and put it to use. It can use the money to expand operations, buy new equipment, hire new employees, or pay off old debts. Because the company is publicly owned, the shareholders have a say in everything the company does.

Yahoo! made its first public offering on April 12, 1996, pricing its shares at $13 each. By the time trading was finished, lucky investors saw the stock (YHOO on NASDAQ) rise to $33, meaning they had more than doubled their money. By the end of the day, Yahoo!, which until then had been nowhere close to being a billion-dollar company, was valued at $850 million. The company's forty-nine employees, most of whom had stock of their own, had hit an instant gold mine.

Yahoo! sales director Mike Nelson *(center left)* joins Chicago Board Options Exchange president and CEO William J. Brodsky *(center right)* and colleagues to celebrate the opening moments of trading for Yahoo! options on September 9, 1997. Becoming a publicly traded company was a big step for Yahoo!, as the move brought with it plenty of much-needed cash.

Thanks to the hundreds of investors who felt Yahoo! held promise, the company had found the money to stay afloat. Yang and Filo had become virtual multimillionaires overnight. Their hard work had paid off, and now they just had to keep things rolling.

GROWTH AND PROFITS

Over the years, Yahoo! continued to grow in popularity, and with that growth came more profits. Advertising brought in most of the cash, but so did business relationships with companies like MCI, which established Yahoo! as an Internet service provider, or ISP. Now people could not only use Yahoo! as a search engine, they could also use it to connect to the Internet in the first place. Yahoo! also began posting links to online stores. This was an easy way to make money. They charged the stores to list their sites on the Yahoo! page, and every time a surfer clicked on one of those sites and bought something from the store, Yahoo! took part of the profit.

Not surprisingly, Yahoo! grew like mad. Its stock price went up, and investors stayed happy. Yang, Filo, and many of the company's employees grew rich. By 1998, more than 1 million people used the site every day.

Yahoo! headquarters are now in Sunnyvale, California. Today, the company makes much of its money through advertising. Advertising on the Yahoo! Web site is worthwhile for businesses because its heavy traffic guarantees plenty of exposure. Yahoo! earns hundreds of millions of dollars every year, a fact that makes both its employees and its shareholders extremely happy.

Meanwhile, with the company growing at a rapid rate, moves were made to improve office conditions. First, they moved from their original headquarters in Mountain View to Sunnyvale, a suburb just south of San Francisco and north of San Jose. When they outgrew those offices, they moved to another location in Sunnyvale about a mile down the road. With each move, the Yahoo! team brought with them their strong work ethic. They put in long hours, but they never forgot to have fun. From the start, they organized bowling teams, ultimate Frisbee teams, a softball team, and intensely competitive foosball tournaments. The games were a great distraction—exactly what people needed when they were so devoted to their work.

CHAPTER FOUR

TODAY'S YAHOO!

Yang and Filo's project has become a huge success story. From its humble beginnings as the first online navigational guide to the Web, the company has grown to become one of the biggest, most successful businesses ever to emerge from California's Silicon Valley.

Today, Yahoo! has more than 7,500 employees. Some of the early executives, including Tim Koogle, have moved on to different jobs, but many of the original innovators remain. What also remains is the company's philosophy of making work not only productive, but fun. Employees, who continue to spend long hours in their offices, also find time to play on-the-job games like basketball, volleyball, and even dodgeball. To fuel all that hard work and good fun, an onsite cafeteria keeps everyone well fed.

Yahoo! continues to surf the leading wave of innovation. Toward that end, it continually upgrades its site, offering more and more features to better meet the needs of its users. Entertainment, especially, has become a big feature on the site. Yahoo! constantly supplies discerning users with features that bring everything a person would expect from TV, radio, and computers into one place.

STAYING SHARP

The Internet has come a long way since it was first developed, and today there are all kinds of online services available for consumers. Not surprisingly, Yahoo! has quite a bit of competition to deal with. America Online, the company that initially tried to buy Yahoo! out, is one of those competitors. Google, the online search engine that recently held a public stock offering of its own, is another. With companies like these constantly evolving to meet surfers' demands,

A man in the North Beach section of San Francisco gives the new Yahoo! Local Internet-enabled bus stop kiosk a try in 2004. The kiosk, the first of its kind in the world, featured an Internet-connected forty-two-inch (107 centimeter) plasma monitor, a keyboard, and a printer that people could use to print maps and other useful information.

Yahoo! is forced to keep a sharp eye on all the latest trends and make sure it doesn't get left behind. The Yahoo! team is in a high-pressure business, and no one wants to fail.

Keeping up with the latest trends is one of Yahoo!'s biggest jobs. "I think that we are inventing a new business model here where it involves a little bit media, a little bit of commerce," Yang explained to the *Motley Fool Radio Show* in early 1999. "We will absolutely have to stay ahead of what our users want and be able to continue to bring them services and products that make sense."[1]

One of the ways Yahoo! has been successful in this regard is by acquiring more than twenty other Internet companies, including GeoCities and HotJobs. Yahoo! bought these companies because they offered services Yahoo! wanted to offer itself, plus they already had devoted users. By purchasing them, Yahoo! achieved two goals. They eliminated the competition, and they gained new users and instant credibility.

THE CRASH OF 2000

One of Yang and Filo's greatest challenges has been surmounting the crash of 2000. In March

THE CRASH OF 2000

Besides inflated stocks, many factors contributed to the dot-com bubble finally bursting. After several years of unchecked economic growth, investors were given pause when, in 2000, the U.S. government found Microsoft in violation of antitrust laws.

Antitrust laws were established in the United States in the late nineteenth century. Competition is a cornerstone of the U.S. economy, and antitrust laws gave the government the right to intervene if a business was trying to gain an illegal advantage over their competitors.

Antitrust laws also made monopolies illegal. A business is considered to be a monopoly when it becomes so large that smaller businesses can no longer compete with it. The U.S. government ruled that Microsoft had become a monopoly and that it would have to change some of its business practices.

Although this ruling didn't have a great impact on Microsoft, it made investors nervous. It also coincided with the aftermath of Y2K. Y2K was a widespread programming glitch that resulted in many computer programs being unable to process a certain date—namely, the year 2000. The international news media ran story after story about Y2K, predicting disastrous computer problems around the world. People were afraid that computers would crash on January 1, 2000. Many businesses, as well as the federal government, invested a lot of money in new equipment and computer experts in order in prepare for Y2K. This spending gave a large boost to the economy.

After 2000, however, many businesses had a lot of brand-new computer equipment. They would not need to buy any more for quite some time. Spending slowed down, and the economy leveled out.

Once the dot-com market lost its momentum, stock values plunged. The crash began in March 2000 and did not end until October 2002. The NASDAQ, which had hit a high of 5,132.52, fell all the way to 1,108.49—an overall decline of 78 percent. A lot of people lost their jobs, and investors suddenly found that they owned stock that was virtually worthless. All told, more than $8 trillion was lost in the crash.

2000, the NASDAQ—the technology stock exchange on which Yahoo! traded—hit an all-time high of 5,132.52. That number seemed to be a sure sign that technology companies were doing great.

If you looked a little more closely, however, many of the companies' stock values were much higher than they should have been, considering the success they'd had as businesses. Some stockbrokers called this phenomenon a bubble and said stocks were inflated. They thought the stocks were overvalued and would inevitably come crashing down. The bubble, they said, would pop.

The bubble did pop soon after that March 2000 high point, and California's Silicon Valley was hit especially hard. Silicon Valley is full of technology companies. Many had gone public, selling their stock to the public in order to raise money. When the market crashed, dropping in value almost 80 percent over two years, these companies went down with it.

Yahoo!, unfortunately, wasn't immune to the fall. Before the crash of 2000, Yahoo!'s shares traded at $230 each. After the dot-com bubble popped, the stock fell to about $8. The value of Yahoo! as a company was just a fraction of what it had been.

Unlike a lot of other companies, Yahoo! didn't fold. Instead, Yahoo!'s management took a hard look at the way the company was set up and made some big changes. Hundreds of employees were laid off, new managers were hired, and advertisers were sought who could bring in new money. Before long, the company was well on its way to recovery. Many of the dot-com businesses of the mid- to late '90s were destroyed by the crash of 2000. Yahoo!'s survival is a sure sign it's doing something right.

GOING GLOBAL

Yahoo! has come a long way since the days when Yang and Filo spent countless sleepless nights in their leaky California office. Today, the company has offices not only in the United States but also

⬆ Yahoo! has grown from a search engine based out of Stanford University to a global business with branches all over the world. This man puts the finishing touches on an advertisement for Yahoo! China in Beijing. Countries like China offer potentially limitless business opportunities to Internet companies like Yahoo!.

in Europe, Asia, Latin America, Australia, and Canada. As of 2005, there are international versions of Yahoo! in twenty-five countries and thirteen different languages. Yahoo!'s global traffic has reached an average of 3 billion page views per day. More than 345 million people use Yahoo! every month. Some studies suggest this may be the largest audience to visit any Web site. With all that traffic, Yahoo! continues to make money as well, turning large profits ($840 million in 2004) while many other Internet companies sink into debt and ruin.

LOTS OF SERVICES

When Yang and Filo started Yahoo!, it was just a search engine. People used it to find their favorite Web sites or to find interesting new ones. Today, however, Yahoo! offers much more. The company considers itself a "Web portal," a place where people can come to do all kinds of things. There's a search engine, of course, but Yahoo! also offers an e-mail service, a bill-pay service, digital photography services, a yellow-pages service, travel services, and numerous other handy features for both consumers and businesses. Businesses can log on to Yahoo! and use the portal to help them communicate with employees, customers, and shareholders. People looking for music can find thousands of offerings at Yahoo!. Those looking for movies can do the same.

Yang and Filo, along with the Yahoo! team, realized that this is what people want. They want one-stop shopping, to be able to find everything in one place, where it is easy to reach, easy to understand, and easy to use. The philosophy is simple: with the world at their fingertips, every-one will be happy. As Yang told *Metroactive*, Yahoo! was made to succeed: "We've designed this for people who like to explore the Net, for people who know what they want but also for people who want to know what is there. And we've built it to last."[2]

IN IT FOR THE LONG HAUL

One of the reasons Yang and Filo were so suc-cessful with their business is they were devoted to a superior product. They didn't take the early get-rich-quick offers from other companies, and they stuck to their guns as their company grew. "We really weren't into this for the money or for the fast payoff," Filo told the *Metroactive* inter-viewer. "There is a great tradition of people

Computer courses are now a standard part of the curriculum in many high schools and universities worldwide. Computer-savvy students can expect plenty of job opportunities when they graduate from school, as many companies are in constant need of skilled workers with high-tech know-how.

around here starting companies and then sticking around long enough to grow them. That's what we are after. We hope to be around for a long time."[3]

CHAPTER FIVE

CHANGING THE WORLD

With Yahoo!, Jerry Yang and David Filo changed the way the world sees media. They brought the world to people's computers, allowing them to conveniently access limitless amounts of information. Internet technology existed before Yahoo!, but an easy way to put that technology to work did not. Yang and Filo's business has evolved with the Internet, embracing the latest inventions in online technology, such as broadband and wireless connections, and harnessing those inventions to make Yahoo! even better.

Both men have gradually taken on new roles at Yahoo!, leaving much of the operation of the company to their trusted employees. Filo now serves as a Yahoo! technologist, using all of the experience he picked up as a student and entrepreneur to oversee the technical details behind Yahoo!'s day-to-day operation. For his part, Yang is now serving on the Yahoo! board of directors. He also works closely with Yahoo!'s current president and CEO, doing what he can to develop innovative business strategies that will keep Yahoo! on the cutting edge of Internet media and communications.

Not surprisingly, Yang and Filo have not announced any plans to return to Stanford University's electrical engineering department to finish their Ph.D.s. Both men are in their late 30s, and both are quite well off (they're each worth somewhere between two and three billion dollars). School, at this point, is a distant memory. Either could retire right this second and never have to work another day of his life. But today, years after it all began, they continue on, most likely because they enjoy it. The Internet, after all, was their hobby from the start.

YAHOO! IN CHINA

China, a country of more than one billion people, is the next big market for Internet companies like Yahoo!. However, there is no freedom of speech in China, and the Internet is censored by the Chinese government. Those who try to get around that censorship face severe punishment.

Consider what happened to the Chinese journalists Shi Tao, Li Zhi, and Jiang Lijun. According to Chinese authorities, they posted information online that was critical of the Chinese government. Chinese court records indicate that Yahoo! supplied information about the writers' Yahoo! e-mail accounts. That information was then used to link the journalists to their online postings and was critical to their convictions. Although the company denies that it did anything wrong, some people have since called for a boycott of Yahoo!.

It remains to be seen what will ultimately happen with the three journalists and whether Yahoo! will be cleared of accusations that it collaborated with Chinese authorities. Meanwhile, the case has made one thing very clear: the worldwide spread of the Internet, and the freedom of speech it promises, has a long way to go.

TEN YEARS AND COUNTING

In March 2005, Yang and Filo celebrated Yahoo!'s ten-year anniversary by ringing the opening bell

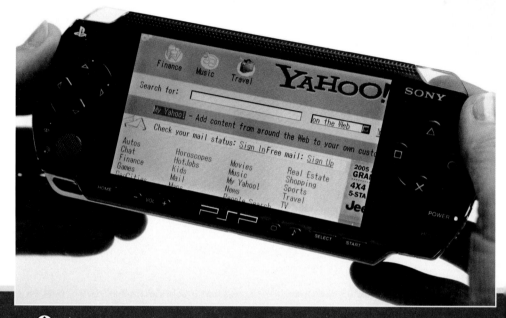

🎧 There is more than one way to access the Internet. Some people use the Sony PlayStation Portable, which allows them to surf the Internet from just about anywhere. Thanks to portable gadgets like this, Yahoo! has found an audience among those on the go.

for the NASDAQ exchange and by offering Yahoo! visitors a free scoop of Baskin-Robbins ice cream (a coupon was available on the company Web site). Each man also gave his thoughts on what they'd gone through and where they're most likely headed. Yang, for one, said he'd had a great time as a Chief Yahoo.

"In just one decade," said Yang, "the Internet has changed the way consumers do just about everything—and it's been a remarkable and wonderful experience. Through it all, we wanted to build products that satisfied our users' wants and needs, but it's even more than that—it's to help every one of us to discover, get more done, share, and interact."[1]

Filo stuck to the task at hand—mainly, eating ice cream. "Technology is now easier and more accessible for the 'everyman,' and Yahoo!'s employees play a huge part in that," said Filo. "One of the primary food groups for many Yahoo! employees is ice cream—and we'd like to raise a cone alongside all those who have made Yahoo! a nice place to stay on the Internet."[2]

During the celebration, Yang and Filo spoke at a press conference, again recounting their time spent in charge of one of the Internet's most successful companies. "It feels like a blink," said Yang. "The time has gone by very quickly. Yahoo! is a constant work in progress. We don't want to look back too much, because you can lose sight of the future."[3]

And this time, Filo got down to business, bringing up the fact that they'd built Yahoo!

Jerry Yang poses with former U.S. president Bill Clinton at the China Internet Summit in Hangzhou, China, in September 2005. Internet commerce in China is in its early stages, much as it was in the United States in the mid-1990s.

PIONEERS

Yang and Filo have never let their success go to their heads. They are humble, hardworking guys who are devoted to the company they created.

In 2005, Yahoo!'s chairman and CEO, Terry Semel, said in an interview with the Associated Press, "They are the pioneers, the guys who have made it possible for us to do the things that had never been done before. But it's not like they walk into work acting like this is the company that they started. They are always looking at what they can do as part of the team to make Yahoo! more relevant in people's lives."[4]

from a relatively small company to a huge one, and that now the big test would be to get to that next level. "It's immensely more challenging to get to $10 billion in revenue than it was to get to $10 million in revenue," Filo said. "That's why we are still here today. The problems have gotten harder, the challenges have gotten bigger, and it's gotten more exciting."[5]

"In some ways, it feels like we have been doing this for as long as we can remember," said Filo. "But in other ways, it feels like we are still at the beginning. Ten years from now, things are going to look vastly different."[6]

To celebrate its tenth anniversary in 2005, Yahoo! offered Internet surfers a free scoop of Baskin-Robbins ice cream. From their early years at Stanford University to the present day, Jerry Yang and David Filo have been among the Internet's greatest innovators. They show no signs of stopping any time soon.

Yang and Filo started Yahoo! because they were passionate about the Internet and all it could offer. And in that regard, nothing has changed. They're still working hard, still defining the cutting edge of Internet commerce. In all likelihood, they'll be at the top for a long time to come.

TIMELINE

1958— President Eisenhower creates ARPA in response to the Soviet Union's launch of *Sputnik*.

1962— J. C. R. Licklider's conceptual Galactic Network becomes the model for the future Internet.

1965— Lawrence Roberts and Thomas Merrill use a telephone line to connect computers in Massachusetts and California.

1969— In the earliest form of the Internet, the ARPANET successfully links four host computers in different parts of the West.

1972— ARPANET technology is demonstrated to the public for the first time.

The first e-mail message is sent.

1988— David Filo earns his BS degree in computer engineering from Tulane University.

1989— Scientists at McGill University in Montreal invent Archie, the world's first Internet site-indexing software.

TIMELINE

1990— Jerry Yang earns his BS and MS degrees in electrical engineering from Stanford University.

1991— University of Minnesota scientists invent the Gopher search system.

The World Wide Web is invented at CERN in Geneva, Switzerland.

1992— Delphi becomes the first commercial Internet service provider; AOL, Prodigy, and CompuServe soon follow.

Marc Andreessen and researchers at the University of Illinois invent Mosaic.

Filo and Yang begin using the Internet and dabbling with e-mail and newsgroups.

January 1994— Yang and Filo create Jerry and David's Guide to the World Wide Web.

February 1994— The guide reaches 100 Web page catalogs. On their personal computers in a borrowed campus trailer, Yang and Filo make a list of their favorite

(continued on following page)

TIMELINE

(continued from previous page)

sites and group them by categories and subcategories.

April 1994— Yang and Filo put their list online for their friends to use.

May 1994— One hundred thousand Internet users access the Yahoo! site.

March 2, 1995— Yahoo! is incorporated.

April 1995— Sequoia Capital provides Yahoo! with an initial investment of $2 million.

April 12, 1996— Yahoo! goes public.

October 1, 1996— Yahoo!'s traffic reaches 1 billion page views.

November 10, 1997— Yahoo!'s U.S. audience grows to 25 million users.

1997–present— Yahoo! acquires many companies and launches new services throughout the world.

2000— Technology stock bubble bursts; stock market crashes.

December 2001— Yahoo! acquires HotJobs, a leading employment service Web site.

2003— Stock market begins its recovery.

TIMELINE

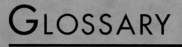

GLOSSARY

Archie The first software to automatically collect and file Internet sites, creating a searchable list.

ARPA Advanced Research Projects Agency; an agency of the U.S. Department of Defense created by President Dwight D. Eisenhower in the late 1950s to help the United States develop its technological abilities.

ARPANET The earliest version of the Internet; the ARPANET was a project of the Advanced Research Projects Agency.

consumer A person who uses the services of a business.

data Information.

database A collection of data organized in such a way that it is easy to access and understand.

digital Having to do with numbers; digital technology uses data in the form of numbers to compress a large amount of information into a compact and usable format.

digital subscriber line (DSL) A modern, high-speed service allowing users to access the Internet over phone lines.

dissertation The final research paper a student has to submit in order to earn a doctoral degree.

e-commerce Short for "electronic commerce," e-commerce is business done on the Internet.

entrepreneur A person who starts up a new business.

gopher A type of search engine designed to scan local networks.

infrastructure The basic structure of a network or a system.

initial public offering (IPO) Used in reference to the first time a business offers its stock to the public for purchase.

Internet A global network connecting computers and other networks worldwide. The World Wide Web is part of the Internet.

multimedia A combination of different means of communication, such as the Internet, telephone, television, and radio.

network Two or more computers connected electronically. The Internet is the world's largest network.

operating system The primary program on a computer, upon which all other programs run.

pioneer A person who leads the way into previously unexplored territory.

portal An entrance or doorway; an Internet portal is a place people can go to access the Internet.

revenue The total income of a business.

search engine An interface to a Web server that categorizes and organizes Web pages into an easy-to-search format.

server A central computer that stores Web pages.

software Computer programs.

spider A software robot that acts as a search engine, following links around the Internet to automatically retrieve information.

UNIX A computer operating system developed in the early 1970s. Favored by computer programmers, UNIX is not often used by the average person.

venture capitalist A person who invests money to help a new business in return for partial ownership of that business.

visionary A person with great imagination, especially when it comes to predicting what the world will need or look like in the future.

Web site A location on the World Wide Web. A Web site generally consists of a number of related Web pages that may contain text, graphics, and multimedia files.

World Wide Web Also known as the Web, a part of the Internet containing Web pages made using HTML (hypertext markup language).

FOR MORE INFORMATION

American Computer Museum
2304 North 7th Avenue, Suite B
Bozeman, MT 59715
(406) 582-1288
Web site: http://www.compustory.com

Computer History Museum
1401 N. Shoreline Boulevard
Mountain View, CA 94043
(650) 810-1010
Web site: http://www.computerhistory.org

National Air and Space Museum
6th and Independence Avenue SW
Washington, DC 20560
(202) 633-1000
Web site: http://www.nasm.si.edu

Netscape World Headquarters
P.O. Box 7050
Mountain View, CA 94039-7050
(650) 254-1900
Web site: http://channels.netscape.com/ns/
  info/default.jsp

Yahoo! Inc.
701 First Avenue
Sunnyvale, CA 94089
(408) 349-3300
Web site: http://www.yahoo.com

WEB SITES

Due to the changing nature of Internet links, the
Rosen Publishing Group, Inc., has developed an
online list of Web sites related to the subject of this
book. This site is updated regularly. Please use this
link to access the list:

http://www.rosenlinks.com/icb/jydf

FOR FURTHER READING

Angel, Karen. *Inside Yahoo! Reinvention and the Road Ahead*. New York, NY: John Wiley & Sons, 2002.

Hock, Randolph. *Yahoo! to the Max: An Extreme Searcher Guide*. Medford, NJ: Cyberage Books/Information Today, 2005.

Neibaur, Alan. *How to Do Everything With Yahoo!*. Berkeley, CA: Osborne Publishing, 2000.

Entrepreneur.com. "How to Build a Million Dollar Business—Yahoo! Unconventional Thinking." Retrieved April 26, 2005 (http://www.entrepreneur.com/Magazines/Copy_of_MA_SegArticle/0,4453,227589----10-,00.html).

Hedger, Jim. "Yahoo! Turns 10." *StepForth News*, March 2, 2005. Retrieved April 26, 2005 (http://news.stepforth.com/2005-news/Yahoo-Turns-10.shtml).

Howe, Walter. "A Brief History of the Internet." Retrieved May 4, 2005 (http://www.walthowe.com/navnet/history.html).

Kopytoff, Verne. "It Started as Two Guys in a Trailer: Yahoo Stands as One of Internet's Biggest Success Stories." *San Francisco Chronicle*, February 28, 2005. Retrieved April 28, 2005 (http://www.sfgate.com/cgi-bin/article.cgi?file=/chronicle/archive/2005/02/28/BUGJUBGR5D1.DTL&type=business).

Leiner, Barry M. "A Brief History of the Internet." Internet Society. Retrieved May 4, 2005 (http://www.isoc.org/internet/history/brief.shtml).

Liedtke, Michael. "Yahoo's Legacy: Profits Are Possible on the Internet." TechnologyReview.com,

February 28, 2005. Retrieved April 26, 2005 (http://www.technologyreview.com/articles/05/02/ap/ap_3022805.asp?p=0).

Plotkin, Hal. "A Couple of Yahoos." *Metroactive*, April 1996. Retrieved April 2005 (http://www.metroactive.com/papers/metro/04.11.96/yahoo-9615.html).

Stanford University School of Engineering. "Jerry Yang and David Filo." Retrieved April 26, 2005 (http://soe.stanford.edu/AR95-96/jerry.html).

Wawro, Thaddeus. *Radicals and Visionaries: Entrepreneurs Who Revolutionized the 20th Century*. Irvine, CA: Entrepreneur Press, 2000

SOURCE NOTES

CHAPTER 2

1. Hal Plotkin, "A Couple of Yahoos," *Metroactive*, April 1996. Retrieved April 2005 (http://www.metroactive.com/papers/metro/04.11.96/yahoo-9615.html).

2. Tom Gardner and David Gardner, "Motley Fool Radio Interview with Yahoo! Co-founder Jerry Yang," *Motley Fool Radio Show*, March 3, 1999. Retrieved April 2005 (http://www.fool.com/specials/1999/sp990303yanginterview.htm).

3. Ibid.

4. Plotkin.

5. Verne Kopytoff, "It Started as Two Guys in a Trailer: Yahoo Stands as One of Internet's Biggest Success Stories," *San Francisco Chronicle*, February 28, 2005. Retrieved April 28, 2005 (http://www.sfgate.com/cgi-bin/article.cgi?file=/chronicle/archive/2005/02/28/BUGJUBGR5D1.DTL&type=business).

6. Plotkin.

7. Gardner and Gardner.

8. Stanford University School of Engineering, "Jerry Yang and David Filo." Retrieved April 2005 (http://soe.stanford.edu/AR95-96/jerry.html).

CHAPTER 3

1. Stanford University School of Engineering, "Jerry Yang and David Filo." Retrieved April 2005 (http://soe.stanford.edu/AR95-96/jerry.html).

2. Hal Plotkin, "A Couple of Yahoos," *Metroactive*, April 1996. Retrieved April 2005 (http://www.metroactive.com/papers/metro/04.11.96/yahoo-9615.html).

CHAPTER 4

1. Tom Gardner and David Gardner, "Motley Fool Radio Interview with Yahoo! Co-founder Jerry Yang," *Motley Fool Radio Show*, March 3, 1999. Retrieved April 2005 (http://www.fool.com/specials/1999/sp990303yanginterview.htm).

2. Hal Plotkin, "A Couple of Yahoos," *Metroactive*, April 1996. Retrieved April 2005 (http://www.metroactive.com/papers/metro/04.11.96/yahoo-9615.html).

3. Ibid.

Chapter 5

1. Yahoo!, "Get the Scoop! Yahoo! Celebrates Ten Years on the Internet with Free Ice Cream," March 2, 2005. Retrieved April 2005 (http://docs.yahoo.com/docs/pr/release1218.html).

2. Ibid.

3. Michael Liedtke, "Yahoo's Legacy: Profits Are Possible on the Internet," TechnologyReview.com, February 28, 2005. Retrieved April 26, 2005 (http://www.technologyreview.com/articles/05/02/ap/ap_3022805.asp?p=0).

4. Michael Liedtke, "Yahoo Turns 10," CBS News.com, February 28, 2005. Retrieved April 2005 (http://www.cbsnews.com/stories/2005/02/28/tech/main677057.shtml).

5. Liedtke, "Yahoo's Legacy: Profits Are Possible on the Internet."

6. Verne Kopytoff, "It Started as Two Guys in a Trailer: Yahoo Stands as One of Internet's Biggest Success Stories," *San Francisco Chronicle*, February 28, 2005. Retrieved April 28, 2005 (http://www.sfgate.com/cgi-bin/article.cgi?file=/chronicle/archive/2005/02/28/BUGJUBGR5D1.DTL&type=business).

INDEX

About the Author

Michael Weston is a writer and photographer. E-commerce and the people behind the Internet's most successful online businesses are a favorite subject of his. His last book on the topic covered the emerging world of e-commerce and Internet security. Weston lives in upstate New York.

Photo Credits

Cover, pp. 3, 44 Yahoo!; cover and interior pages graphic element © Royalty-Free/Corbis; pp. 6, 57, 60 © Ed Kashi/Corbis; p. 9 © Time & Life Pictures/Getty Images; p. 13 © Michael Nicholson/Corbis; p. 17 © Reuters/Corbis; p. 20 © Roger Ressmeyer/Corbis; p. 26 © Ed Quinn/Corbis; p. 35 © Gerald French/Corbis; p. 40 Courtesy of the National Center for Supercomputing Applications (NCSA) and the Board of Trustees of the University of Illinois; p. 48 © Jon Levy/AFP/Getty Images; p. 55 © Adam Lubroth/Getty Images; p. 59 © Eric Sander/Getty Images; pp. 64, 68, 70, 79 (bottom), 86 © AP/Wide World Photos; p. 74 © Kim Kulish/Corbis; p. 82 © Tom Stewart/Corbis; p. 88 © AP/WWP/WCPV; p. 90 © Business Week/Getty Images.

Designer: Nelson Sá
Photo Researcher: Jeffrey Wendt